Autumn Splendor
Adult Coloring Book

An Adult Coloring Book Featuring Fun and Relaxing Autumn Scenes with Pumpkins, Flowers, Cute Animals and Much More!

Copyright 2021 © Coloring Book Cafe
All Rights Reserved.

**Copyright @ 2021 Coloring Book Cafe
All Rights Reserved.**

All rights reserved. No part of this publication may be reproduced or used in any form or by any means graphic, electronic, or mechanical, including photocopying, recording, or information storage-and-retrieval without permission of the publisher.

The designs in this book are intended for the personal, noncommercial use of the retail purchaser and are under federal copyright laws; they are not to be reproduced in any form for commercial use. Permission is granted to photocopy content for the personal use of the retail purchaser.

an Imprint of **The Fruitful Mind Publishing LTD.**
www.coloringbookcafe.com

Have questions? Let us know.
support@coloringbookcafe.com

This Book Belongs To:

Find the digital version of this title &
many more digital releases on:

www.digitalbookcafe.com

COLOR CHART

WWW.COLORINGBOOKCAFE.COM

Printed in Great Britain
by Amazon